Prim

PLACI

MW01702908

Specific Skill Series for Language Arts

Mechanics

Leveled Books in Nine Key Language Arts Skill Areas

SRA

Columbus, OH

The McGraw-Hill Companies

Cover: ©PhotoDisc/Getty Images, Inc.

SRAonline.com

SRA

Send all inquiries to:
SRA/McGraw-Hill
8787 Orion Place
Columbus, OH 43240-4027

Printed in the United States of America.

ISBN 0-07-601739-7

1 2 3 4 5 6 7 8 9 MAZ 08 07 06 05 04

TO THE TEACHER

ABOUT THE *PLACEMENT TESTS*

Teachers can use the *Placement Tests* for each skill area to determine how to place students in the appropriate level of the program. There are three test levels: Primary, Intermediate, and Advanced. Each test level includes two forms of tests—Form X and Form Y. Either form may be used as a pretest for student placement or a posttest to measure student progress. The following chart can be used as a guide for determining which test level to administer to each student.

Test Level	Appropriate for Students at Level. . .
Primary	A, B, or C (Grades 1–3)
Intermediate	D, E, or F (Grades 4–6)
Advanced	G or H (Grades 7–8)

Primary and Intermediate tests are each twelve pages long, and Advanced tests are eight pages long to allow for accurate assessment of students' skill levels. The tests consist of representative pages selected from the Student Editions; four pages are selected from each level, as shown on the chart below. Teachers may, if they wish, administer only four pages of a test at a time to determine if a student should advance to the next level.

Test Level	Page Numbers	Selected from Level. . .	Test Level	Page Numbers	Selected from Level. . .
Primary Form X	6–9	A	Primary Form Y	40–43	A
	10–13	B		44–47	B
	14–17	C		48–51	C
Intermediate Form X	18–21	D	Intermediate Form Y	52–55	D
	22–25	E		56–59	E
	26–29	F		60–63	F
Advanced Form X	30–33	G	Advanced Form Y	64–67	G
	34–37	H		68–71	H

INSTRUCTIONS FOR USING THE *PLACEMENT TESTS*

1. Students should be instructed to turn to the page corresponding to the level and form of the test that is to be administered. The tests are not designed to be timed, but teachers may choose to set a time limit for the completion of a test.
2. Students should record their answers on the worksheet found in the back of this book or on separate pieces of paper. No answer should be recorded in the *Placement Test* books.
3. Check students' answers using the Answer Keys in the *Teacher's Manual,* and use the scale below as a guide for placement if administering the entire test.

Test Level	Score	Placement Level
Primary	lower than 40%	A
	40%–79%	B
	80% or higher	C (or D if score is 98% or higher)
Intermediate	lower than 40%	D
	40%–79%	E
	80% or higher	F (or G if score is 98% or higher)
Advanced	lower than 75%	G
	75% or higher	H

TABLE OF CONTENTS
PLACEMENT TESTS FORM X

Specific Skill Series
for Language Arts
Mechanics

PLACEMENT TESTS

FORM X
Primary
Intermediate
Advanced

PRIMARY—FORM X
Test begins on this page.

A Nice Visit

Which part of the sentence is missing a capital letter? If no capital letters are missing, choose *None.*

1. Erica and I | visited Maine. None
(A) (B) (C)

---

2. our flight was | five hours long. None
(A) (B) (C)

---

3. We went | to see grandpa. None
(A) (B) (C)

---

4. We had | picnics and planted flowers. None
(A) (B) (C)

---

5. We walked | his dog sam. None
(A) (B) (C)

Summer

Which sentence is written correctly?

6. **(A)** Summer is here and we will be busy.

(B) summer is here and we will be busy.

7. **(A)** On monday we get our pool passes.

(B) On Monday we get our pool passes.

8. **(A)** Then my sister karen needs a swimsuit.

(B) Then my sister Karen needs a swimsuit.

9. **(A)** She grew out of her suit last august.

(B) She grew out of her suit last August.

10. **(A)** Karen and I can swim on Tuesday.

(B) Karen and i can swim on Tuesday.

11. **(A)** I wish we could take our dog felix.

(B) I wish we could take our dog Felix.

Which sentence's end mark is correct?

12. **(A)** Send me the card.
(B) Send me the card?

---

13. **(A)** Where is the clock.
(B) Where is the clock?

---

14. **(A)** It is so cold?
(B) It is so cold!

---

15. **(A)** Who owns this truck.
(B) Who owns this truck?

---

16. **(A)** Please wash your hands?
(B) Please wash your hands.

---

17. **(A)** Tell me where to go.
(B) Tell me where to go?

---

18. **(A)** I cannot wait for summer!
(B) I cannot wait for summer?

Choose the sentence that follows the rules for using capital letters and end marks.

19. **(A)** This is our teacher's new desk
(B) His old desk was small?
(C) It came on Thursday.

20. **(A)** Does Nancy have the lock!
(B) Did I give it to her in February?
(C) i lost the key.

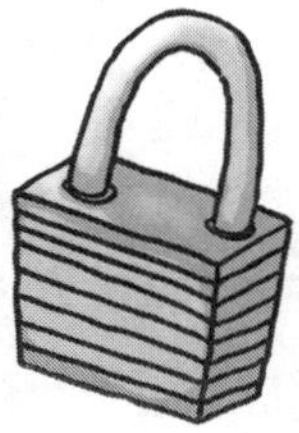

21. **(A)** Mom said aunt helen got a dog.
(B) I am so excited!
(C) What did she name the dog!

22. **(A)** He planted flowers in March.
(B) Where did he plant them!
(C) they are in the front yard.

My Book

Which sentence is written correctly?

23. **(A)** I am writing a book called *Holiday in space*.
(B) I am writing a book called *Holiday in Space.*

24. **(A)** In my book, Captain Ace is the hero.
(B) In my book, captain Ace is the hero.

25. **(A)** He flies all the way to Pluto.
(B) he flies all the way to Pluto.

26. **(A)** Captain Ace's helper is his dog, Yipper.
(B) Captain Ace's helper is his dog, yipper.

27. **(A)** He and His Dog live in memphis.
(B) He and his dog live in Memphis.

28. **(A)** I hope mr. Gonzalez will read it to the class.
(B) I hope Mr. Gonzalez will read it to the class.

Water

Is the end mark correct in each sentence?

29. We are learning about water.
(A) Yes **(B)** No

30. What do you know about water.
(A) Yes **(B)** No

31. Do all living things need water?
(A) Yes **(B)** No

32. Water carries nutrients through your body!
(A) Yes **(B)** No

33. Oh, that water is cold!
(A) Yes **(B)** No

34. Do you drink enough water.
(A) Yes **(B)** No

Which sentence shows the correct way to use commas?

35. **(A)** I cannot tell the difference between frogs, and toads.
(B) Can you find Irving, Texas, on the map?
(C) The dry crackly, leaves crunched under our feet.

---

36. **(A)** "Lee has not read the book yet" said Matt.
(B) I cannot be there until Tuesday November, 17.
(C) My cat meows at birds, but she does not chase them.

---

37. **(A)** I will call you, when I am done or I will get a ride home with Ken.
(B) "Early Americans," I said, "chewed gum made from beeswax."
(C) Elise moved to 25113 Eaton Avenue Northfield, Minnesota.

---

38. **(A)** The birdhouse kit included wood, screws, and sandpaper.
(B) The first Thanksgiving was held on December, 18, 1777.
(C) "I cannot find my other shoe" complained, Jack.

---

39. **(A)** We packed pillows books, and notebooks for the bus trip.
(B) I was quiet but the, turtles all plopped into the pond.
(C) Thursday, May 18, is the day of the concert.

Math Workshop

Which sentence shows the correct way to use quotation marks?

40. **(A)** Mrs. Blake said, "Stack your tiles" in groups of ten.
(B) Mrs. Blake said", Stack your tiles in groups of ten."
(C) Mrs. Blake said, "Stack your tiles in groups of ten."

---

41. **(A)** Does anyone have any tiles left over? "she asked."
(B) "Does anyone have any tiles left over? she asked."
(C) "Does anyone have any tiles left over?" she asked.

---

42. **(A)** "I have some, said Kurt, that I can add to Rita's."
(B) "I have some," said Kurt, "that I can add to Rita's."
(C) "I have some, said Kurt," that I can add to Rita's."

---

43. **(A)** "We can make another stack of ten! cheered Rita.
(B) "We can make another stack of ten!" cheered Rita.
(C) "We can make another stack of ten!" "cheered Rita."

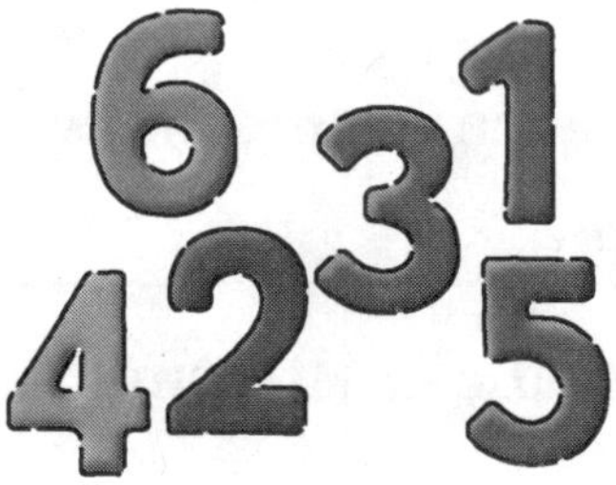

With Grandpa

Which part of the sentence is missing a capital letter? If no capital letters are missing, choose *None.*

44. My grandfather is a | CEO, which stands for | chief executive officer. | None
(A) My grandfather is a
(B) CEO, which stands for
(C) chief executive officer.
(D) None

45. He knows four | languages, including German, | French, and russian. | None
(A) He knows four
(B) languages, including German,
(C) French, and russian.
(D) None

46. On labor Day | he took me | to his office. | None
(A) On labor Day
(B) he took me
(C) to his office.
(D) None

47. He said i should | start learning | what grown-ups do. | None
(A) He said i should
(B) start learning
(C) what grown-ups do.
(D) None

48. First, we rode the | elevator with pete, who | cleans the offices. | None
(A) First, we rode the
(B) elevator with pete, who
(C) cleans the offices.
(D) None

49. Then, grandpa | showed me | his office. | None
(A) Then, grandpa
(B) showed me
(C) his office.
(D) None

50. I saw | the photograph that | uncle Louie had taken of the family. | None
(A) I saw
(B) the photograph that
(C) uncle Louie had taken of the family.
(D) None

51. I could see | most of the city | from the office window. | None
(A) I could see
(B) most of the city
(C) from the office window.
(D) None

Read each envelope. Look at the underlined words. Decide how periods should be used.

(52) <u>Ms Roberta Cortez</u>
(53) <u>1350 Porter Pl</u>
Keller, TX 76244

(54) <u>Mr. and Mrs Hackney</u>
(55) <u>883 Mast Bl.vd</u>
Keller, TX 76244

52. **(A)** MS. Roberta Cortez
(B) M.S. Roberta Cortez
(C) Ms. Roberta Cortez
(D) Correct as it is

---

53. **(A)** 1350 Porter PL
(B) 1350 Porter Pl.
(C) 1350 Porter P.
(D) Correct as it is

---

54. **(A)** Mr and Mrs. Hackney
(B) M.r. and Mrs. Hackney
(C) Mr. and Mrs. Hackney
(D) Correct as it is

---

55. **(A)** 883 Mast Blvd.
(B) 883 Mast Bl.Vd.
(C) 883 Mast BVD.
(D) Correct as it is

Read each letter. Look at the underlined words. Decide how colons should be used.

May 3, 2005

(56) <u>Dear Mrs. Taylor</u>

Here is some information for you to consider as you plan your field trip to our farm. It takes us **(57)** <u>until 830</u> to finish morning chores. In the afternoon, we start chores at **(58)** <u>about 300</u>. We have the following young animals **(59)** <u>on the farm lambs, goats, chicks, calves, and piglets.</u> We look forward to Friday the twenty-seventh.

Until then,
Mrs. Linda Kurt

56. **(A)** Dear: Mrs. Taylor
(B) Dear Mrs.: Taylor
(C) Dear Mrs. Taylor:
(D) Correct as it is

---

57. **(A)** until 8:30
(B) until :830
(C) until 830:
(D) Correct as it is

---

58. **(A)** about 30:0
(B) about 3:00
(C) about 300:
(D) Correct as it is

---

59. **(A)** on: the farm lambs, goats, chicks, calves, and piglets.
(B) on the farm: lambs, goats, chicks, calves, and piglets.
(C) on the: farm lambs, goats, chicks, calves, and piglets.
(D) Correct as it is

Read each letter. Look at the underlined words. Decide how capital letters and punctuation should be used.

February 19, 2005

(60) Dear superintendent Rivas

My third-grade class would like to visit the waste disposal site in Lincoln County. If possible, we would like to make our trip during the week of March 15. Our visit would be sometime **(61)** between 1000 A.M. and 2:00 P.M. Please let us know if that is okay. You may reply to me at Cove Central Elementary, **(62)** State Route 74, Edmond Oklahoma 73013.

Sincerely,
Tisha Vincent

60. **(A)** Dear Superintendent Rivas:
(B) Dear superintendent Rivas:
(C) Dear Superintendent Rivas
(D) Correct as it is

---

61. **(A)** between 1000: A.M. and 2:00 P.M.
(B) between 1:000 A.M. and 2:00 P.M.
(C) between 10:00 A.M. and 2:00 P.M.
(D) Correct as it is

---

62. **(A)** State Route 74 Edmond Oklahoma, 73013
(B) State Route 74, Edmond, Oklahoma 73013
(C) State Route 74, Edmond Oklahoma, 73013
(D) Correct as it is

PRIMARY—FORM X ends on this page.

INTERMEDIATE—FORM X
Test begins on this page.

Which part of the sentence is missing a capital letter? If no capital letters are missing, choose *None.*

1. The Fraternal Order (A) | of alaska state troopers, or F.O.A.S.T., (B) | has a museum in Anchorage. (C) | None (D)

2. The Ymca (A) | in my city (B) | offers rooms for travelers. (C) | None (D)

3. Can you guess (A) | where the girl scouts celebrate (B) | World Thinking Day? (C) | None (D)

4. I have to go (A) | to another store (B) | to buy speedy sneakers. (C) | None (D)

5. My father (A) | is a CPA, or certified public accountant, (B) | in Indiana. (C) | None (D)

6. The national audubon society (A) | has chapters in (B) | every state. (C) | None (D)

7. The sierra club's (A) | main office is (B) | in San Francisco. (C) | None (D)

8. Dazzle jeans (A) | are on sale (B) | at dunham's department store. (C) | None (D)

Neighbors

Read the envelope below. Look at the underlined parts. Decide how periods should be used.

(9) P S Shears
(10) 381 Prescott Rd.
Northport, ME 04849

Mr. Steven Weeden
(11) 722 Yorkland Ct
(12) Northport, ME. 04849

9. (A) P S. Shears
(B) P. S. Shears
(C) P. S Shears
(D) Correct as it is

10. (A) 381 Prescott Rd
(B) 381 Prescott Ro.
(C) 381 Prescott R.
(D) Correct as it is

11. (A) 722 Yorkland Crt
(B) 722 Yorkland C.
(C) 722 Yorkland Ct.
(D) Correct as it is

12. (A) Northport, M. E. 04849
(B) Northport, ME 04849
(C) Northport, M. E 04849
(D) Correct as it is

City Park

Which sentence uses commas correctly?

13. **(A)** In the afternoon, the park is especially busy.
(B) In the afternoon the park is, especially busy.
(C) In the, afternoon the park is especially busy.

---

14. **(A)** Near the bridge children, are jumping rope.
(B) Near the bridge, children are jumping rope.
(C) Near, the bridge children are jumping rope.

---

15. **(A)** Under the evergreen trees students, collect pine needles.
(B) Under the evergreen trees, students collect pine needles.
(C) Under the evergreen trees students collect, pine needles.

---

16. **(A)** Beside the fountain dogs, run and splash.
(B) Beside the, fountain dogs run and splash.
(C) Beside the fountain, dogs run and splash.

---

17. **(A)** In the distance you can, see skyscrapers.
(B) In the distance you, can see skyscrapers.
(C) In the distance, you can see skyscrapers.

---

18. **(A)** On the pavement children play, hopscotch.
(B) On the pavement, children play hopscotch.
(C) On the pavement children, play hopscotch.

---

19. **(A)** During the hottest part of the day, the tar bubbles on the sidewalk.
(B) During, the hottest part of the day the tar bubbles on the sidewalk.
(C) During the hottest, part of the day the tar bubbles on the sidewalk.

---

20. **(A)** After four o'clock the park is, almost empty.
(B) After four o'clock, the park is almost empty.
(C) After four o'clock the park, is almost empty.

Media Mania

Is underlining used correctly in each sentence?

21. I think I've read Redwall six times.
(A) Yes **(B)** No

---

22. I have seen The Lion King movie, but not the play.
(A) Yes **(B)** No

---

23. My mother has The Wall Street Journal delivered to her office.
(A) Yes **(B)** No

---

24. My grandmother bought me a subscription to Dig because she knows I enjoy archaeology.
(A) Yes **(B)** No

---

25. My drama teacher is casting The Sound of Music tomorrow.
(A) Yes **(B)** No

---

26. My cousin has tickets to see Man of La Mancha on Broadway.
(A) Yes **(B)** No

---

27. The Chicago Tribune's slogan is "World's Greatest Newspaper."
(A) Yes **(B)** No

---

28. Movie actor Katharine Hepburn starred in The Philadelphia Story in 1940.
(A) Yes **(B)** No

---

29. The setting of Where the Red Fern Grows is the Ozarks of northeastern Oklahoma.
(A) Yes **(B)** No

---

30. Muse is a magazine for young people who are interested in science.
(A) Yes **(B)** No

INTERMEDIATE—FORM X

In which part of each sentence is there a capitalization error? If there is not an error, choose *None*.

	(A)	(B)	(C)	(D)
31.	I hope I can stay up	until midnight	on new year's eve.	None
32.	The space needle	in Seattle is a	popular tourist attraction.	None
33.	The Pentagon is one	of this country's	largest office buildings.	None
34.	This week's	read-aloud book	is *A walk in the woods.*	None
35.	Mom remembers	hearing her grandparents	speak russian.	None
36.	Tickets for the movie	*Time stands Still*	are sold out.	None
37.	The origins of buddhism	can be traced	to India.	None
38.	The audience applauded	for the actor's	first emmy Award.	None
39.	The poem	"One Snowflake"	is brief and simple.	None
40.	Is a copy of	the declaration of independence	in this museum?	None
41.	One of my family's	thanksgiving traditions	is to volunteer.	None

Which sentence uses commas correctly?

42. **(A)** The boys went to the fair and they had a good, time.
(B) The boys went to the fair, and they had a good time.
(C) The boys went to the fair and, they had a good time.

---

43. **(A)** This festival offers food, dancing, and workshops.
(B) This festival offers food dancing, and workshops.
(C) This festival offers food, dancing and workshops.

---

44. **(A)** The sight of the golden, chilled pudding made us hungry.
(B) The sight of the, golden chilled pudding made us hungry.
(C) The sight of the golden chilled, pudding made us hungry.

---

45. **(A)** The sun was shining but, I still felt cold.
(B) The sun was shining but I still, felt cold.
(C) The sun was shining, but I still felt cold.

---

46. **(A)** Where are my keys, hat and wallet?
(B) Where are my keys, hat, and, wallet?
(C) Where are my keys, hat, and wallet?

---

47. **(A)** Dad drove the car, or, it is in the shop.
(B) Dad drove the car, or it is in the shop.
(C) Dad, drove the car or it is in the shop.

---

48. **(A)** Is that poem by Poe, Blake, or Wordsworth?
(B) Is that poem by Poe, Blake, or, Wordsworth?
(C) Is that poem by Poe, Blake or Wordsworth?

The Business Trip

Which sentence uses a colon, a semicolon, or a hyphen correctly?

49. **(A)** Tara Caldwell's flight was late there; was a delay in Denver.
(B) Tara Caldwell's flight; was late there was a delay in Denver.
(C) Tara Caldwell's flight was late; there was a delay in Denver.

---

50. **(A)** Her plane did not land until 9:38 A.M.
(B) Her plane did not land until 93:8 A.M.
(C) Her plane did not land until: 938 A.M.

---

51. **(A)** Tara's luggage could not be found on-the-ever-revolving luggage rack.
(B) Tara's luggage could not be found on the ever-revolving-luggage rack.
(C) Tara's luggage could not be found on the ever-revolving luggage rack.

---

52. **(A)** Tara claimed the following: lost items one suitcase, one briefcase, and one garment bag.
(B) Tara claimed the following lost items: one suitcase, one briefcase, and one garment bag.
(C) Tara claimed: the following lost items one suitcase, one briefcase, and one garment bag.

---

53. **(A)** Luckily, Tara held her portfolio with all thirty-one designs.
(B) Luckily, Tara held her portfolio with all-thirty one designs.
(C) Luckily, Tara held her portfolio with all thirty-one-designs.

---

54. **(A)** Tara saw a man with her name; on a sign she was relieved.
(B) Tara saw a man; with her name on a sign she was relieved.
(C) Tara saw a man with her name on a sign; she was relieved.

---

55. **(A)** Dean Nelson spent forty-five-minutes with Tara.
(B) Dean Nelson spent forty-five minutes with Tara.
(C) Dean Nelson spent forty five-minutes with Tara.

Which sentence uses dashes, parentheses, ellipses points, and apostrophes correctly?

56. **(A)** I will send that file (from last week once) I have reviewed it.
(B) I will send that file (from last week once I) have reviewed it.
(C) I will send that file (from last week) once I have reviewed it.

---

57. **(A)** Did he read pages 7–15?
(B) Did he read pages–7–15?
(C) Did he read pages 7–15–?

---

58. **(A)** "Friends, Romans, Countrymen . . ." is the beginning to a well-recognized speech from history.
(B) "Friends, Romans, Countrymen . . ." . . . is the beginning to a well-recognized speech from history.
(C) "Friends, Romans, Countrymen" . . . is the beginning to a well-recognized speech from history.

---

59. **(A)** Devin hopes shel'l get a part in the ballet.
(B) Devin hopes she'll get a part in the ballet.
(C) Devin hopes sh'ell get a part in the ballet.

---

60. **(A)** Hand me—your clay—projects slowly as you leave the classroom today.
(B) Hand me your clay projects—slowly—as you leave the classroom today.
(C) Hand me your clay projects slowly as—you leave—the classroom today.

---

61. **(A)** William (Randolph) Hearst 1863–1951 published newspapers.
(B) William Randolph Hearst (1863–1951 published) newspapers.
(C) William Randolph Hearst (1863–1951) published newspapers.

---

62. **(A)** Marcus wondered if the coat on the hanger was yours.
(B) Marcus wondered if the coat on the hanger was your's.
(C) Marcus wondered if the coat on the hanger was yours'.

Which part of the sentence contains an error in capitalization? If there is no error, choose *None.*

63. If you visit the south, | you may see landmarks | of the Civil War. | None
(A) (B) (C) (D)

64. The largest county | in wisconsin | is Marathon County. | None
(A) (B) (C) (D)

65. It's hard to imagine | woolly mammoths | once roamed west Virginia. | None
(A) (B) (C) (D)

66. Florida has many laws | to protect its variety | of wild animals. | None
(A) (B) (C) (D)

67. John Adams was | the first president to live in | the white house. | None
(A) (B) (C) (D)

68. If you travel out West, | you must see | the grand canyon. | None
(A) (B) (C) (D)

69. The Port of baltimore | is a port of entry | for foreign-made cars. | None
(A) (B) (C) (D)

70. When you | are in cullman, Alabama, check out | the Bluegrass Super Jam. | None
(A) (B) (C) (D)

71. The Carlsbad caverns | in New Mexico are a | popular tourist attraction. | None
(A) (B) (C) (D)

72. This weekend my town | is holding its annual | Founder's Day Parade. | None
(A) (B) (C) (D)

Which sentence uses commas and quotation marks correctly?

73. **(A)** Clay asked, “What do we do if she’s not here?”
(B) Clay asked “What, do we do if she’s not here?”
(C) Clay asked “,What do we do if she’s not here?”

---

74. **(A)** “Let’s just wait, and see” said Keisha.
(B) “Let’s just wait and see,” said Keisha.
(C) “Let’s, just wait and see said Keisha.”

---

75. **(A)** “Maybe we should keep studying”, said Clay “just in case she’s here.”
(B) “Maybe, we should keep studying”, said Clay, “just in case she’s here.”
(C) “Maybe we should keep studying,” said Clay, “just in case she’s here.”

---

76. **(A)** “Gee that’s just, what I was thinking, said Tommy,” rolling his eyes.
(B) “Gee that’s, just what I was thinking, said Tommy, rolling his eyes.”
(C) “Gee, that’s just what I was thinking,” said Tommy, rolling his eyes.

---

77. **(A)** “I, on the other hand have an even better idea, claimed Pat.”
(B) “I on the other hand, have an even, better idea,” claimed Pat.
(C) “I, on the other hand, have an even better idea,” claimed Pat.

---

78. **(A)** “We could, of course, work on our art projects until Mrs. Kable gets here,” he suggested.
(B) “We could, of course, work on our art projects until Mrs. Kable gets here”, he suggested.
(C) “We could, of course work on our art projects, until Mrs. Kable gets here,” he suggested.

---

79. **(A)** “Good morning students” said Mrs. Kable from the open doorway.
(B) “Good morning, students,” said Mrs. Kable from the open doorway.
(C) “Good morning students”, said Mrs. Kable from the open doorway.

Choose the answer that shows the correct use of quotation marks.

80. (A) "Now who wants to share the title of his or her own poem with the class, asked Ms. Berry?"
(B) Now who wants to share the title of his or her own poem with the class?" asked Ms. Berry
(C) "Now who wants to share the title of his or her own poem with the class?" asked Ms. Berry.

---

81. (A) Aaron walked to the front of the room and wrote "An Ode to My Toad" on the board.
(B) "Aaron walked to the front of the room and wrote An Ode to My Toad on the board."
(C) Aaron walked to the front of the room and wrote "An Ode to My Toad on the board.

---

82. (A) Mika's poem "title, Stinky Cheese and Hot Dogs, Please", made Fred giggle.
(B) Mika's poem title, "Stinky Cheese and Hot Dogs, Please," made Fred giggle.
(C) Mika's poem title, Stinky Cheese and Hot Dogs, Please", made Fred giggle.

---

83. (A) Christian's poem was titled The Wind "That Blows between a Hippo's Toes."
(B) Christian's poem was titled "The Wind That Blows between a Hippo's Toes."
(C) Christian's poem was titled "The Wind That Blows between" a Hippo's Toes.

---

84. (A) "I must say," said Ms. Berry with a laugh, "these are some of the strangest titles I've ever heard!"
(B) "I must say, said Ms. Berry with a laugh, "these are some of the strangest titles I've ever heard!"
(C) "I must say", said Ms. Berry with a laugh, these are some of the strangest titles I've ever heard!"

Choose the answer that shows the correct use of dashes, parentheses, ellipses, and apostrophes.

85. **(A)** I'll send you today's assignment (unless you already got it from Miss Berg.
(B) I'll send you today's assignment (unless you already got it from Miss Berg.)
(C) I'll send you today's assignment (unless you already got it from Miss Berg).

---

86. **(A)** This traffic jam—and it is the worst I've ever seen—delayed us for forty-five minutes.
(B) This traffic jam and it is—the worst I've ever seen—delayed us for forty-five minutes.
(C) This traffic jam—and it is the worst I've ever seen delayed us for forty-five minutes.

---

87. **(A)** How many people know that the Gettysburg Address includes the words "The brave men, . . . who struggled here, have consecrated it"?
(B) How many people know that the Gettysburg Address includes the words ". . . The brave men, . . . who struggled here, have consecrated it"?
(C) How many people know that the Gettysburg Address includes the words "The brave men, . . . who struggled here, have consecrated it . . ."?

---

88. **(A)** The Iverson's havent stopped raking leaves all morning.
(B) The Iversons have'nt stopped raking leaves all morning.
(C) The Iversons haven't stopped raking leaves all morning.

---

89. **(A)** (Maize) the West Indian name for corn is an important food source in Mexico.
(B) Maize the West Indian name for corn is an (important food source) in Mexico.
(C) Maize (the West Indian name for corn) is an important food source in Mexico.

---

90. **(A)** Actor, comedian, and author Bill Cosby stated, . . . "The very first law in advertising is . . . to cultivate the delightfully vague."
(B) Actor, comedian, and author Bill Cosby stated, "The very first law in advertising is . . . to cultivate the delightfully vague. . ."
(C) Actor, comedian, and author Bill Cosby stated, "The very first law in advertising is . . . to cultivate the delightfully vague."

INTERMEDIATE—FORM X ends on this page.

ADVANCED—FORM X

Test begins on this page.

Which item corrects the capitalization error in each sentence?

1. The organization called american association of retired persons is known as AARP for short.

(A) American Association of Retired Persons
(B) The Organization called
(C) known as aarp
(D) Correct as it is

---

2. The Meredith foundation gives money to many projects in education and the arts.

(A) The Meredith Foundation
(B) gives money to many Projects
(C) in Education and the Arts
(D) Correct as it is

---

3. The members of the track team all wear running shoes made by fleet feet.

(A) The Members of the track team
(B) all wear Running Shoes
(C) by Fleet Feet
(D) Correct as it is

---

4. Look at all these great bargains I found when I went shopping at s mart.

(A) these Great Bargains
(B) i found
(C) at S Mart
(D) Correct as it is

---

5. The Ecology Club in our town is starting to publish a weekly newspaper called *The green sheets on Main Street.*

(A) ecology Club
(B) Our Town
(C) *The Green Sheets on Main Street*
(D) Correct as it is

Choose the answer that shows where the comma or commas should be.

6. Letisha, Beth, Anna and Megan are running in the relay.
(A) Letisha, Beth, Anna, and Megan are running in the relay.
(B) Letisha, Beth, Anna and Megan, are running in the relay.
(C) Correct as it is

---

7. I really wanted to see the hurdles event but I arrived too late.
(A) I really wanted to see the hurdles event but, I arrived too late.
(B) I really wanted to see the hurdles event, but I arrived too late.
(C) Correct as it is

---

8. Rahmid is a fast sprinter isn't he?
(A) Rahmid is a fast, sprinter isn't he?
(B) Rahmid is a fast sprinter, isn't he?
(C) Correct as it is

---

9. Ella is a timer at the event, and Jessica records results.
(A) Ella is a timer at the event and Jessica, records results.
(B) Ella is a timer at the event and Jessica records results.
(C) Correct as it is

---

10. The third runner in the relay was fast, but he did not pass the baton well.
(A) The third runner in the relay was fast but he did not pass the baton well.
(B) The third runner in the relay was fast but he, did not pass the baton well.
(C) Correct as it is

---

11. The tired, sweaty, runners poured water on their faces.
(A) The tired, sweaty runners poured water on their faces.
(B) The tired sweaty, runners poured water on their faces.
(C) Correct as it is

---

12. We watched cheered, and clapped for hours at the meet.
(A) We watched, cheered, and clapped for hours at the meet.
(B) We watched, cheered and clapped for hours at the meet.
(C) Correct as it is

The New Crew

Choose the correct way to write the underlined part of each sentence. The underlined part may or may *not* require hyphens.

13. Members of the Zoo Crew assembled in the newly renovated zoo office at 1:30 P.M.
(A) in the newly renovated-zoo office
(B) in the newly renovated zoo-office
(C) Correct as it is

---

14. In all, there were twenty two-new Crew members.
(A) twenty two new Crew-members
(B) twenty-two new Crew members
(C) Correct as it is

---

15. Most of the volunteers had experience working with zoo animals before.
(A) working with zoo-animals before
(B) working-with-zoo animals before
(C) Correct as it is

---

16. The-ever-popular assignment choices were the chimpanzees, the tigers, the eagles, and the sharks.
(A) The ever popular assignment-choices
(B) The ever-popular assignment choices
(C) Correct as it is

---

17. "Some Zoo Crew members think of themselves as foster parents of a zoo animal," said Ms. Romano with a room brightening smile.
(A) with a room brightening-smile
(B) with a room-brightening smile
(C) Correct as it is

ADVANCED—FORM X

Which part of the sentence contains an error in capitalization or punctuation? If there is no error, choose *None.*

18. Andie gave her report | on greenland | to the class yesterday. | None
(A) (B) (C) (D)

19. That jet airplane | is one of the world's | fastest isn't it? | None
(A) (B) (C) (D)

20. Spring and fall | —they're both seasons | of change are my favorites. | None
(A) (B) (C) (D)

21. Do you think aunt Margie | will ask me to be | in her wedding? | None
(A) (B) (C) (D)

22. What Edgar is thinking | of doing, strikes me | as a terrible idea! | None
(A) (B) (C) (D)

23. Memorial Day | always seems like the | first day of summer. | None
(A) (B) (C) (D)

24. The exhibits | include: | lions, seals, and gorillas. | None
(A) (B) (C) (D)

25. Toni Morrison, | an African American novelist won | the Nobel Prize in 1993. | None
(A) (B) (C) (D)

26. Ben tugged on the video, | but it wouldn't come out | of the V.C.R. | None
(A) (B) (C) (D)

ADVANCED—FORM X

In which part of each sentence is there a capitalization error? If there is no error, choose *None.*

	(A)	(B)	(C)	(D)
27.	Individual liberties	are protected	by the Bill of Rights.	None
28.	Muhammad,	the founder of islam,	was born in Arabia in A.D. 500.	None
29.	The folksinger invited	us to sing along	on "down in the valley."	None
30.	Because of the fog,	we could not see	the statue of liberty.	None
31.	Two of the visitors	speak swahili	very well.	None
32.	That picture book received	the Caldecott medal	last year.	None
33.	Monica reviewed	the film *double duty*	in the school newspaper.	None
34.	Labor day celebrations	in our town have changed	over the years.	None
35.	There are	thirty-five million knots	in the *Ardabil Carpet*.	None
36.	We saw	her rushing to her	economics 101 class.	None
37.	The golden gate bridge	opened to traffic	on May 28, 1938.	None
38.	Who	wrote	"when Lilacs last in the Dooryard bloomed"?	None
39.	On our summer vacation,	we visited the	tomb of the Unknowns.	None

Choose the answer that shows where the comma or commas should be. In some cases, no commas are needed.

40. I'd like to go get a lemonade but I don't want to miss any of the match.
(A) I'd like to go get a lemonade, but I don't want to miss any of the match.
(B) I'd like to go get a lemonade but, I don't want to miss any of the match.
(C) Correct as it is

---

41. Roddick has a great serve, doesn't he?
(A) Roddick has a great serve doesn't he?
(B) Roddick has a great, serve doesn't he?
(C) Correct as it is

---

42. The sizzling well-placed serve was an ace.
(A) The sizzling, well-placed serve was an ace.
(B) The sizzling well-placed, serve was an ace.
(C) Correct as it is

---

43. Blake is down forty-love in this game but I think he can make a comeback.
(A) Blake is down forty-love in this game but I think, he can make a comeback.
(B) Blake is down forty-love in this game, but I think he can make a comeback.
(C) Correct as it is

---

44. The players traded points but neither one could get far ahead.
(A) The players traded points, but neither one could get far ahead.
(B) The players traded points but neither one, could get far ahead.
(C) Correct as it is

---

45. A group of eager, sunburned fans waited outside the locker room.
(A) A group of eager sunburned fans waited outside the locker room.
(B) A group of eager sunburned, fans waited outside the locker room.
(C) Correct as it is

---

46. One player signed autographs, and another posed for a photo.
(A) One player signed autographs and another posed for a photo.
(B) One player signed autographs and, another posed for a photo.
(C) Correct as it is

Science Friday

Which item shows the correct way to punctuate the underlined part of the sentence? In some cases, punctuation is not needed.

47. I was very excited about the Science Fair my project had been completed for over a week.
(A) I was very excited about the Science Fair: my project
(B) I was very excited about the Science Fair; my project
(C) Correct as it is

48. About one half of the projects had to do with biology.
(A) About one half-of the projects
(B) About-one half of the projects
(C) Correct as it is

49. The longest caterpillar in James's study measured two and one-eighth inches.
(A) measured two and-one-eighth inches.
(B) measured two and one eighth-inches.
(C) Correct as it is

50. Brad's project was a design for a more fuel efficient car.
(A) design for a more fuel-efficient car.
(B) design for a more fuel efficient-car.
(C) Correct as it is

51. Tammy tested different bug repellents, including three well known brands.
(A) including three well-known-brands.
(B) including three well-known brands.
(C) Correct as it is

52. Zoe watered bean plants with three kinds of water rainwater, distilled water, and tap water.
(A) with three kinds of water;
(B) with three kinds of water:
(C) Correct as it is

53. This fabric can be hazardous it catches fire easily.
(A) This fabric can be hazardous; it catches fire easily.
(B) This fabric can be hazardous: it catches fire easily.
(C) Correct as it is

54. One judge asked this question: "How is wind powered electricity generated?"
(A) asked this question: "How is wind-powered electricity generated?"
(B) asked this question: "How is wind powered-electricity generated?"
(C) Correct as it is

Which sentence shows the correct use of quotation marks?

55. Marcos summarized an article entitled "A Breath of Fresh Air."
(A) Marcos summarized an article "entitled A Breath of Fresh Air."
(B) Marcos summarized an article entitled A Breath of Fresh Air.
(C) Correct as it is

---

56. Amanda enjoyed the story "Zlateh the Goat" by Isaac Bashevis Singer.
(A) Amanda enjoyed the story Zlateh "the Goat" by Isaac Bashevis Singer.
(B) Amanda enjoyed the "story Zlateh the Goat" by Isaac Bashevis Singer.
(C) Correct as it is

---

57. "After dark," she said, "we'll tell stories around the campfire."
(A) After dark," she said, "we'll tell stories around the campfire.
(B) "After dark, she said, we'll tell stories around the campfire."
(C) Correct as it is

---

58. The most famous song in that musical is Send in the Clowns.
(A) The most famous song in that musical is "Send in the Clowns."
(B) The "most famous song" in that musical is Send in the Clowns.
(C) Correct as it is

---

59. The best chapter in the book was "Escape from Griswald Mountain."
(A) The best chapter in the "book was "Escape from Griswald Mountain."
(B) The best chapter in the "book" was Escape from Griswald Mountain.
(C) Correct as it is

---

60. Joyce's favorite song is Sounds of Silence by Simon and Garfunkel.
(A) Joyce's favorite song is Sounds of Silence by "Simon and Garfunkel."
(B) Joyce's favorite song is "Sounds of Silence" by Simon and Garfunkel.
(C) Correct as it is

ADVANCED—FORM X ends on this page.

TABLE OF CONTENTS
PLACEMENT TESTS FORM Y

Specific Skill Series
for Language Arts
Mechanics

PLACEMENT TESTS

FORM Y

Primary
Intermediate
Advanced

Art Class

Which part of the sentence is missing a capital letter? If no capital letters are missing, choose *None.*

1. My teacher's name | is Mr. cooper. | None
(A) (B) (C)

2. he said that we | have a special task. | None
(A) (B) (C)

3. We will paint | each other's picture. | None
(A) (B) (C)

4. My painting partner | is patrick. | None
(A) (B) (C)

5. i will paint | Mr. Cooper's picture too. | None
(A) (B) (C)

Which sentence is written correctly?

6. **(A)** We have a surprise to finish by july.
   (B) We have a surprise to finish by July.

---

7. **(A)** Karen and I help Dad for the parade.
   (B) Karen and I help dad for the parade.

---

8. **(A)** he is making a float.
   (B) He is making a float.

---

9. **(A)** The parade is on a Saturday morning.
   (B) The parade is on a saturday morning.

---

10. **(A)** We will ask Mom if she needs a ride.
    (B) We will ask mom if she needs a ride.

---

11. **(A)** The float will be in front of our house.
    (B) the float will be in front of our house.

Which sentence's end mark is correct?

12. **(A)** Are we late.
(B) Are we late?

---

13. **(A)** The book is due next Friday.
(B) The book is due next Friday!

---

14. **(A)** She takes the bus to school?
(B) She takes the bus to school.

---

15. **(A)** What are they building.
(B) What are they building?

---

16. **(A)** Take your time on the test.
(B) Take your time on the test?

---

17. **(A)** I love my gift?
(B) I love my gift!

Choose the sentence that follows the rules for using capital letters and end marks.

18. **(A)** Is that yours!
(B) That is my old crib.
(C) Why is it for sale.

---

19. **(A)** The fan is not broken.
(B) It will get hot in july.
(C) we will need a fan.

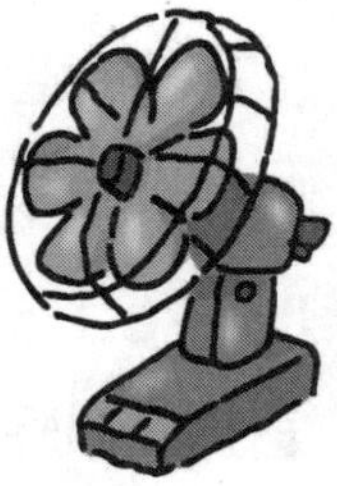

---

20. **(A)** I like to watch birds?
(B) it must be fun to fly.
(C) Birds are great!

---

21. **(A)** What did he eat for breakfast!
(B) Does he like cereal?
(C) He will have toast and juice too

---

22. **(A)** When do you practice.
(B) I practice on Tuesdays and Sundays.
(C) I love to play the flute?

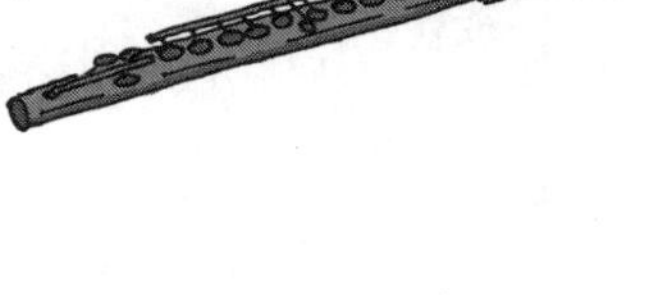

Which sentence is written correctly?

23. **(A)** We cook out on the Fourth of july.
(B) We cook out on the Fourth of July.

---

24. **(A)** On Memorial day I went to a picnic.
(B) On Memorial Day I went to a picnic.

---

25. **(A)** The Missouri River is the longest river in the United States.
(B) The Missouri River is the longest river in the United states.

---

26. **(A)** Nearly 75% of West Virginia is covered by forests.
(B) Nearly 75% of West virginia is covered by forests.

---

27. **(A)** Do you know who general Lee was?
(B) Do you know who General Lee was?

---

28. **(A)** My birthday is December 13, 1997.
(B) My birthday is december 13, 1997.

---

29. **(A)** Mom works in downtown detroit.
(B) Mom works in downtown Detroit.

Is the end mark correct in each sentence?

30. Many animals live in the water?
(A) Yes **(B)** No

---

31. Look how big that fish is!
(A) Yes **(B)** No

---

32. Do you know what kind it is.
(A) Yes **(B)** No

---

33. Animals and humans need clean water?
(A) Yes **(B)** No

---

34. We can help keep the water clean.
(A) Yes **(B)** No

---

35. You lose water when you perspire.
(A) Yes **(B)** No

---

36. Do you drink six to eight glasses of water a day!
(A) Yes **(B)** No

---

37. Make sure you get enough water to drink?
(A) Yes **(B)** No

Which sentence shows the correct way to use commas?

38. **(A)** "Bring those lights over here," called the director.
(B) Michael Jordan was born on February 17 1963.
(C) Her long, straight, hair hung down to her waist.

---

39. **(A)** The map shows us where the parks, picnic spots and campgrounds are.
(B) Brandon, asked "When do you think Dad will get home?"
(C) Columbus, Georgia, is the second largest city in that state.

---

40. **(A)** "When in doubt" said Mark Twain, "tell the truth."
(B) I knocked on the door but no one answered.
(C) On August 1, 1876, Colorado became a state.

---

41. **(A)** I like to wear old, soft, sneakers.
(B) Toshi went to college in Durham, North Carolina.
(C) Please respond by Tuesday March 25, 2005.

Which sentence shows the correct way to use quotation marks?

42. **(A)** Mrs. Blake told us that the "title of Chapter 4" is Counting by Tens.
(B) Mrs. Blake told us that the title of Chapter 4 is "Counting by Tens."
(C) Mrs. Blake told us that the title of "Chapter 4" is Counting by Tens.

---

43. **(A)** Please "count your tiles by" tens, said Mrs. Blake.
(B) "Please count your tiles by tens," said Mrs. Blake.
(C) "Please count your tiles by tens, said" Mrs. Blake.

---

44. **(A)** Steve announced, "I have eight stacks, so I have 80 tiles.
(B) Steve announced, "I have eight stacks," so I have 80 tiles.
(C) Steve announced, "I have eight stacks, so I have 80 tiles."

---

45. **(A)** It was easy to count by tens," Steve said as he grinned.
(B) "It was easy to count by tens," Steve said as he grinned.
(C) "It was easy to count by tens, Steve said as he grinned."

Which part of the sentence is missing a capital letter? If no capital letters are missing, choose *None.*

46. The florida keys are | a group of islands | south of Florida.
(A) (B) (C)
None
(D)

---

47. The great smoky mountains national park
(A)
| is a popular park | in America.
(B) (C)
None
(D)

---

48. Thousands of people flock | to the Covered bridge festival
(A) (B)
| in Parke County, Indiana.
(C)
None
(D)

---

49. During the period called the great depression,
(A)
| much of Oklahoma was called | the Dust Bowl.
(B) (C)
None
(D)

---

50. In Arvada, Colorado, | families interested in acting
(A) (B)
| can attend family arts day.
(C)
None
(D)

---

51. Utah's rainbow bridge | is the world's
(A) (B)
| largest natural bridge.
(C)
None
(D)

Read each envelope. Look at the underlined words. Decide how periods should be used.

(52) B. G. Edmundson
(53) Hghwy 51
Georgetown, MN 56546

(54) A Paul Spitale
(55) 2208 Brickyard Ct
Georgetown, MN 56546

52. **(A)** B G Edmundson
(B) B. G Edmundson
(C) B G. Edmundson
(D) Correct as it is

---

53. **(A)** Hwy. 51
(B) Hgwy. 51
(C) Hway. 51
(D) Correct as it is

---

54. **(A)** .A Paul Spitale
(B) A. Paul Spitale
(C) A .Paul Spitale
(D) Correct as it is

---

55. **(A)** 2208 Brickyard C.T.
(B) 2208 Brickyard CT.
(C) 2208 Brickyard Ct.
(D) Correct as it is

Read each letter. Look at the underlined words. Decide how colons should be used.

May 14, 2005

(56) Dear Mrs. Kurt

Thank you for letting us visit your farm. We will arrive **(57)** about 940. The children have chosen to learn about **(58)** the following animals lambs, goats, and calves. At 11:15, we will board the bus and return to school. The children are looking forward to the day.

Cordially,
Mrs. Taylor and the third-grade class

56. **(A)** Dear Mrs. Kurt:
(B) Dear: Mrs. Kurt
(C) Dear Mrs.: Kurt
(D) Correct as it is

---

57. **(A)** about: 940
(B) about 9:40
(C) about 94:0
(D) Correct as it is

---

58. **(A)** the following: animals lambs, goats, and calves.
(B) :the following animals lambs, goats, and calves.
(C) the following animals: lambs, goats, and calves.
(D) Correct as it is

Read each letter. Look at the underlined words. Decide how capital letters and punctuation should be used.

March 18, 2005

Dear Lucia,

We had a weird field trip the other day. We went to a landfill. First we saw a movie **(59)** called "Recycling Magic." It showed how they make new things out of old, used-up stuff **(60)** like milk cartons, egg containers and plastic bags. Lucia, did you know that they make park benches out of milk cartons? Anyway, it turned out to be really neat. See you soon.

Your friend,
Tisha

59. **(A)** called "Recycling magic."
(B) called Recycling Magic.
(C) called Recycling Magic.
(D) Correct as it is

---

60. **(A)** like, milk cartons, egg containers and plastic bags.
(B) like milk cartons, egg containers, and plastic bags.
(C) like milk cartons egg containers, and plastic bags.
(D) Correct as it is

PRIMARY—FORM Y ends on this page.

INTERMEDIATE—FORM Y
Test begins on this page.

Which part of the sentence is missing a capital letter? If no capital letters are missing, choose *None*.

1. Visit the World Chess | hall of fame | in Miami, Florida. None
(A) (B) (C) (D)

---

2. The United Nations | is often shortened to | the un. None
(A) (B) (C) (D)

---

3. The oldest university | in the United States | is harvard university. None
(A) (B) (C) (D)

---

4. My uncle started | a snack company called | Creole Cuisine in Louisiana. None
(A) (B) (C) (D)

---

5. Would you like | to join the | explorers club in Kansas? None
(A) (B) (C) (D)

---

6. Do you remember | traveling to visit | the epa headquarters? None
(A) (B) (C) (D)

---

7. This popcorn from | Iowa is called | pop's popcorn. None
(A) (B) (C) (D)

---

8. Groundhog day | is celebrated every | year on February 2. None
(A) (B) (C) (D)

Read the letter below. Look at the underlined parts. Decide how periods should be used.

(9) Mon., Dec 26

(10) Dear Mr Weeden,

I enjoyed our chat the other day. You asked about some of my flowers. Here is the information. I got it from the Maine Tulip Society.

The red tulips grow to about eight inches tall. I purchased them last fall from the **(11)** M.T.S. for nine dollars per dozen plus shipping. I hope we meet again soon.

Sincerely,

(12) Mr Paul S Shears

9. **(A)** Mon Dec 26
(B) Mon, Dec., 26
(C) Mon., Dec. 26
(D) Correct as it is

---

10. **(A)** Dear Mr. Weeden,
(B) Dear MR. Weeden,
(C) Dear M.r. Weeden,
(D) Correct as it is

---

11. **(A)** M.T.S
(B) mts
(C) m.t.s.
(D) Correct as it is

---

12. **(A)** Mr. Paul S Shears
(B) Mr. Paul S. Shears
(C) Mr Paul S. Shears
(D) Correct as it is

The Piano Concert

Which sentence uses commas correctly?

13. **(A)** Seated in, the front row we had a good view of the stage.
(B) Seated in the front row we had, a good view of the stage.
(C) Seated in the front row, we had a good view of the stage.

---

14. **(A)** Pounding the keys loudly, the pianist began the concert.
(B) Pounding the, keys loudly the pianist began the concert.
(C) Pounding the keys loudly the pianist, began the concert.

---

15. **(A)** Amazed we watched his fingers, move at lightning speed.
(B) Amazed we, watched his fingers move at lightning speed.
(C) Amazed, we watched his fingers move at lightning speed.

---

16. **(A)** Leaning in he, hunched his shoulders.
(B) Leaning in, he hunched his shoulders.
(C) Leaning in he hunched, his shoulders.

---

17. **(A)** Mesmerized by the beautiful music, the audience was silent.
(B) Mesmerized by the beautiful, music the audience was silent.
(C) Mesmerized by, the beautiful music the audience was silent.

---

18. **(A)** Finishing with a flourish the pianist stood, and took a bow.
(B) Finishing with a flourish, the pianist stood and took a bow.
(C) Finishing with a, flourish the pianist stood and took a bow.

Is underlining used correctly in each sentence?

19. I haven't read Walk Two Moons yet, so don't tell me the ending!
(A) Yes **(B)** No

---

20. "Did you get a part in Cinderella?" asked Julia.
(A) Yes **(B)** No

---

21. "No," said Michelle in disbelief, "they are doing Sleeping Beauty instead."
(A) Yes **(B)** No

---

22. The New York Times had an interesting article on conservation in last Sunday's edition.
(A) Yes **(B)** No

---

23. My brother didn't read it because he was watching The Apple Dumpling Gang on television.
(A) Yes **(B)** No

---

24. Where did you put my National Geographic World when you were finished reading it?
(A) Yes **(B)** No

---

25. The title of my favorite book is From the Mixed-Up Files of Mrs. Basil E. Frankweiler.
(A) Yes **(B)** No

---

26. Chitty Chitty Bang Bang is about an eccentric inventor who invents a magic car.
(A) Yes **(B)** No

---

27. The Boston Globe has printed the news since 1872.
(A) Yes **(B)** No

In which part of each sentence is there a capitalization error? If there is not an error, choose *None*.

28. Is the name | Steven c. Berg | or Steven T. Berg? None
(A) (B) (C) (D)

29. next week | we will begin | our state history reports. None
(A) (B) (C) (D)

30. Vic asked | general O'Neil about | his training assignment. None
(A) (B) (C) (D)

31. Since his return, | I have not seen | Mr. murphy. None
(A) (B) (C) (D)

32. We think our art teacher, | Mrs. Lombardo, | is the best. None
(A) (B) (C) (D)

33. What does the | saying "a stitch in time | saves nine" mean? None
(A) (B) (C) (D)

34. The sweater i | knitted does | not look even. None
(A) (B) (C) (D)

35. "Can you hear | the cheers from | the arena?" asked Rob. None
(A) (B) (C) (D)

36. Grandma adopted | a cat and | named her flash. None
(A) (B) (C) (D)

37. where is | the index for | this encyclopedia set? None
(A) (B) (C) (D)

38. The nameplate | on this door | reads dr. Priscilla Markson. None
(A) (B) (C) (D)

Which sentence uses commas correctly?

39. **(A)** Dust settled on the floors, window sills, and, walls.
(B) Dust settled on the floors, window sills and walls.
(C) Dust settled on the floors, window sills, and walls.

---

40. **(A)** You can ride your bike, or, you can walk.
(B) You can ride your bike, or you can walk.
(C) You can ride your bike or, you can walk.

---

41. **(A)** Ken Amy and, Savita ride the same bus.
(B) Ken, Amy and Savita ride the same bus.
(C) Ken, Amy, and Savita ride the same bus.

---

42. **(A)** There was just enough flour, sugar, eggs, and corn oil to bake.
(B) There was just enough flour, sugar, eggs and corn oil to bake.
(C) There was just enough flour, sugar eggs, and corn oil to bake.

---

43. **(A)** Most people cannot resist a cute, playful, puppy.
(B) Most people cannot resist a cute, playful puppy.
(C) Most people cannot resist a cute playful, puppy.

---

44. **(A)** There were coupons advertisements, and notices on the board.
(B) There were coupons, advertisements, and notices on the board.
(C) There were coupons, advertisements and, notices on the board.

---

45. **(A)** I would have called sooner, but I woke up late.
(B) I would have called sooner, but, I woke up late.
(C) I would have called sooner but, I woke up late.

---

46. **(A)** Do you have a soft, fluffy, pillow?
(B) Do you have a soft fluffy, pillow?
(C) Do you have a soft, fluffy pillow?

The Interview

Which sentence uses a colon, a semicolon, or a hyphen correctly?

47. **(A)** Nina Kendall was out; of the office her home needed repair.
(B) Nina Kendall was out of the office; her home needed repair.
(C) Nina Kendall was out of; the office her home needed repair.

---

48. **(A)** Kay Goldman was one-quarter of an hour late meeting Tara.
(B) Kay Goldman was one quarter of-an-hour late meeting Tara.
(C) Kay Goldman was one-quarter of an hour late-meeting Tara.

---

49. **(A)** Louis Stilson focused on asking Tara about her exper-
ience.
(B) Louis Stilson focused on asking Tara about her experi-
ence.
(C) Louis Stilson focused on asking Tara about her experie-
nce.

---

50. **(A)** Beth Spano was very interested; in Tara she asked several questions about her portfolio.
(B) Beth Spano was very interested in Tara she asked; several questions about her portfolio.
(C) Beth Spano was very interested in Tara; she asked several questions about her portfolio.

---

51. **(A)** Tara is only three quarters sure she will accept the job-offer.
(B) Tara is only three quarters-sure she will accept the job offer.
(C) Tara is only three-quarters sure she will accept the job offer.

---

52. **(A)** These are Tara's worries company: size, moving, and stability.
(B) These are Tara's: worries company size, moving, and stability.
(C) These are Tara's worries: company size, moving, and stability.

Which sentence uses dashes, parentheses, ellipses points, and apostrophes correctly?

53. **(A)** A (wallaby) an animal in the kangaroo family eats plants.
(B) A wallaby (an animal in the kangaroo family) eats plants.
(C) A wallaby an animal in the kangaroo (family eats plants).

---

54. **(A)** The Berger's enjoy going to the high school's sporting events.
(B) The Bergers enjoy going to the high schools sporting events.
(C) The Bergers enjoy going to the high school's sporting events.

---

55. **(A)** I think it was Picasso who said, . . . A painting is a dramatic action in the course of which reality finds itself split apart.
(B) I think it was Picasso who said, . . . "A painting is a dramatic action in the course of which reality finds itself split apart."
(C) I think it was Picasso who said, ". . . A painting is a dramatic action in the course of which reality finds itself split apart."

---

56. **(A)** The legend of Amelia Earhart (1897–1937) is based partly on her mysterious disappearance.
(B) The legend of (Amelia Earhart) 1897–1937 is based partly on her mysterious disappearance.
(C) The legend of Amelia Earhart—1897–1937—is based partly on her mysterious disappearance.

---

57. **(A)** Those landscapers—though not from this area—have many customers in our neighborhood.
(B) Those landscapers—though not from this area have many customers in our neighborhood.
(C) Those—landscapers—though not from this area have many customers in our neighborhood.

Which part of the sentence contains an error in capitalization? If there is no error, choose *None.*

	(A)	(B)	(C)	(D)
58.	People on our street	always make a float	for the fourth of july parade.	None
59.	On vacation, my family	and I saw the gateway arch	in St. Louis.	None
60.	Few people	have actually read the book	*Bambi: Prince of the forest.*	None
61.	My British ancestors	came to America	and settled in Massachusetts.	None
62.	The movie of	Kipling's *the jungle book*	is far different from the book.	None
63.	The origins of buddhism	go back more than	two thousand years.	None
64.	A tony award	is given for plays on stage,	not for movies.	None
65.	Dad recites	"Casey at the Bat" from memory	at every chance.	None
66.	My family took	their first trip	ever to Niagara falls last month.	None
67.	Great Britain signed	the treaty of Paris	in September 1783.	None
68.	Different kinds	of grass grow in different	areas of the nation.	None

The Morning Routine

Which sentence uses commas correctly?

69. **(A)** In the morning our house, is a busy place.
(B) In the morning, our house is a busy place.
(C) In the morning our house is a busy, place.

---

70. **(A)** After the alarm clock rings, Dad usually gets up first.
(B) After the alarm clock, rings Dad usually gets up first.
(C) After, the alarm clock rings Dad usually gets up first.

---

71. **(A)** Before I do anything else I always, wash my face.
(B) Before I do, anything else I always wash my face.
(C) Before I do anything else, I always wash my face.

---

72. **(A)** By that time, Dad has started making breakfast.
(B) By that time Dad has, started making breakfast.
(C) By that, time Dad has started making breakfast.

---

73. **(A)** On most mornings we all, come downstairs at different times.
(B) On most, mornings we all come downstairs at different times.
(C) On most mornings, we all come downstairs at different times.

---

74. **(A)** From the looks, of our kitchen you'd think a herd of elephants came rumbling through.
(B) From the looks of our kitchen you'd think, a herd of elephants came rumbling through.
(C) From the looks of our kitchen, you'd think a herd of elephants came rumbling through.

---

75. **(A)** In spite of the mess we are always on time and know where everything is.
(B) In spite of the mess, we are always on time and know where everything is.
(C) In spite of the mess we are always on time, and know where everything is.

Which sentence uses colons, semicolons, or hyphens correctly?

76. **(A)** Cliff Markwell's seat; is reserved it is in the center of the front row.
(B) Cliff Markwell's seat is reserved it is in; the center of the front row.
(C) Cliff Markwell's seat is reserved; it is in the center of the front row.

---

77. **(A)** The concert didn't start until 7:37 P.M.
(B) The concert didn't start until 73:7 P.M.
(C) The concert didn't start until: 737 P.M.

---

78. **(A)** The audience grew quiet as the biggest ever student-choir filed onto the stage.
(B) The audience grew quiet as the biggest-ever student choir filed onto the stage.
(C) The audience grew quiet as the biggest-ever-student-choir filed onto the stage.

---

79. **(A)** Following are the teachers who will conduct: the choirs Angie Chou, Juanita Bell, Tim Darcy, and Sam Klopfer.
(B) Following are the teachers who will conduct the choirs: Angie Chou, Juanita Bell, Tim Darcy, and Sam Klopfer.
(C) Following are the teachers: who will conduct the choirs Angie Chou, Juanita Bell, Tim Darcy, and Sam Klopfer.

---

80. **(A)** Fortunately, all twenty seven-singers were able to attend.
(B) Fortunately, all twenty-seven-singers were able to attend.
(C) Fortunately, all twenty-seven singers were able to attend.

---

81. **(A)** It was a hard decision; there was also a track meet on Tuesday night.
(B) It was a hard; decision there was also a track meet on Tuesday night.
(C) It was a hard decision there was; also a track meet on Tuesday night.

---

82. **(A)** Forty-two former students of Mr. Markwell's came to the concert.
(B) Forty two-former students of Mr. Markwell's came to the concert.
(C) Forty-two-former students of Mr. Markwell's came to the concert.

---

83. **(A)** A reception was planned for one half hour after-the-concert.
(B) A reception was planned for one-half hour after the concert.
(C) A reception was planned for one half-hour after the concert.

INTERMEDIATE—FORM Y

Choose the answer that shows the correct use of dashes, parentheses, ellipses, and apostrophes.

84. **(A)** The (ASL Amateur) Storytellers League entertains listeners at their monthly meetings.
(B) The ASL (Amateur Storytellers League) entertains listeners at their monthly meetings.
(C) (The ASL Amateur Storytellers League) entertains listeners at their monthly meetings.

---

85. **(A)** My coffee mug and it is my favorite is a souvenir—from last summer's vacation.
(B) My coffee mug—and it is my favorite—is a souvenir from last summer's vacation.
(C) My coffee mug and—it is my favorite is a souvenir—from last summer's vacation.

---

86. **(A)** The music of Bach 1685–1750 is known (throughout the world) for its beauty and perfection.
(B) The music of (Bach 1685–1750) is known throughout the world for its beauty and perfection.
(C) The music of Bach (1685–1750) is known throughout the world for its beauty and perfection.

---

87. **(A)** Be sure you answer the questions at the end of chapters 6–11 over the weekend.
(B) Be sure you answer the questions at the end of chapters 6 11–over the weekend.
(C) Be sure you answer the questions at the end of chapters–6–11–over the weekend.

---

88. **(A)** A turtle needs it's shell in order to protect itself from predators.
(B) A turtle needs its shell in order to protect itself from predators.
(C) A turtle needs its' shell in order to protect itself from predators.

INTERMEDIATE—FORM Y ends on this page.

ADVANCED—FORM Y
Test begins on this page.

Which part of the sentence includes an error in capitalization? If there is no error, choose *None*.

1. The travel agent spoke (A) | about beautiful gardens (B) | in savannah, Georgia. (C) | None (D)

2. Many people travel (A) | up and down the east coast (B) | by train. (C) | None (D)

3. Robert always tries (A) | to get a front-row seat (B) | at the rose bowl parade. (C) | None (D)

4. The Crow Fair is a five-day event (A) | shared by Native Americans from all over (B) | North America who gather to celebrate their heritage and culture. (C) | None (D)

5. In New York we saw (A) | an exhibit (B) | on the great depression. (C) | None (D)

6. To get to his office, (A) | walk South from the town square (B) | for one block. (C) | None (D)

7. During the Middle Ages (A) | many people traveled (B) | on foot. (C) | None (D)

8. The Yam Festival is (A) | in Ghana, (B) | a country in West Africa. (C) | None (D)

9. I was born in (A) | Richwood, located (B) | in Ohio's Union county. (C) | None (D)

10. Have you ever been (A) | to the Midwest or (B) | to new england? (C) | None (D)

11. There are many (A) | Chinese new year parties (B) | in West Coast cities. (C) | None (D)

Which sentence uses commas correctly?

12. **(A)** "Children please turn off the television, now."
(B) "Children please turn off, the television now."
(C) "Children, please turn off the television now."

---

13. **(A)** "Yes, some networks emphasize light entertainment."
(B) "Yes some, networks emphasize light entertainment."
(C) "Yes some networks emphasize, light entertainment."

---

14. **(A)** "Other networks, though, emphasize news."
(B) "Other networks, though emphasize news."
(C) "Other networks though, emphasize news."

---

15. **(A)** "So do you, prefer dramas or documentaries?"
(B) "So, do you prefer dramas or documentaries?"
(C) "So do you prefer dramas, or documentaries?"

---

16. **(A)** "Well I prefer, dramas."
(B) "Well, I, prefer dramas."
(C) "Well, I prefer dramas."

---

17. **(A)** "Class, please, turn in your television-viewing logs."
(B) "Class please, turn in your television-viewing logs."
(C) "Class, please turn in your television-viewing logs."

---

18. **(A)** "Keisha, you didn't watch any television all week long?"
(B) "Keisha, you didn't watch any television all, week long?"
(C) "Keisha, you didn't watch, any television all week long?"

Read the letter. Look at the underlined parts. Choose the answer that shows the correct use of colons or semicolons.

May 14, 2005

(19) Dear Ms. Romano

Thank you for answering my questions about joining the Zoo Crew volunteer group. **(20)** I am very interested in being part of the group; and I feel I would be a good addition to your crew. I am sending you letters of recommendation **(21)** from the following people

- Art Thomas, a neighbor
- Mr. Charles Leonides, a teacher
- Sergeant Violet Gonzalez, a police officer

I am available for an interview **(22)** anytime after 3:00 on weekdays and Saturdays. You mentioned on the phone that I should list three areas where I would like to work. These are my top three choices **(23)** for assignments; apes, elephants, and penguins. **(24)** My favorite quotation sums up my feelings "Pleasure in the job puts perfection in the work."

(25) I'm very excited about becoming a member of the Zoo Crew; I will phone you next week.

(26) Sincerely

Jason Kim

19. **(A)** Dear: Ms. Romano
(B) Dear Ms. Romano:
(C) Dear Ms. Romano;
(D) Correct as it is

---

20. **(A)** I am very interested in being part of the group: and I feel I would
(B) I am very interested in being part of the group; I feel I would
(C) I am very interested; in being part of the group and I feel I would
(D) Correct as it is

21. **(A)** from the following people:
(B) from the following people;
(C) from: the following people
(D) Correct as it is

---

22. **(A)** anytime after 300:
(B) anytime after 3;00
(C) anytime: after 300
(D) Correct as it is

---

23. **(A)** for assignments: apes: elephants, and penguins.
(B) for assignments: apes, elephants, and penguins.
(C) for: assignments apes, elephants, and penguins.
(D) Correct as it is

---

24. **(A)** My favorite quotation sums up my feelings: "Pleasure in the job puts perfection in the work."
(B) My favorite quotation sums up my feelings; "Pleasure in the job puts perfection in the work."
(C) My favorite quotation sums: up my feelings "Pleasure in the job puts perfection in the work."
(D) Correct as it is

---

25. **(A)** I'm very excited about becoming a member of the Zoo Crew, I will phone you next week.
(B) I'm very excited about becoming a member of the Zoo Crew: I will phone you next week.
(C) I'm very excited; about becoming a member of the Zoo Crew I will phone you next week.
(D) Correct as it is

---

26. **(A)** Sincerely,
(B) Sincerely;
(C) Sincerely:
(D) Correct as it is

Choose the item that shows the correct use of capitalization.

27. We had to walk for several hours to reach the Mayan ruins.
- **(A)** had to Walk
- **(B)** several Hours
- **(C)** to Reach
- **(D)** Correct as it is

---

28. Data-Sure corporation was one of the sponsors of the marathon.
- **(A)** Data-Sure Corporation
- **(B)** was one of the Sponsors
- **(C)** of the Marathon
- **(D)** Correct as it is

---

29. The Daughters of the American revolution, or DAR, gave Kayla an award.
- **(A)** Daughters of the American Revolution
- **(B)** dar
- **(C)** gave Kayla an Award
- **(D)** Correct as it is

---

30. That clothing store carries my favorite brands, including lizzie and sky blue.
- **(A)** That clothing Store
- **(B)** carries my favorite Brands
- **(C)** including Lizzie and Sky Blue
- **(D)** Correct as it is

---

31. Donavan has two free tickets to the concert by the Lancaster Jazz Band.
- **(A)** has two Free tickets
- **(B)** to the Concert by
- **(C)** the Lancaster jazz band
- **(D)** Correct as it is

---

32. The first United States civilian jetliner was flown from New York to Paris.
- **(A)** First United States
- **(B)** Civilian Jetliner
- **(C)** From New York to Paris
- **(D)** Correct as it is

ADVANCED—FORM Y

Choose the answer that shows where the comma or commas should be.

33. So did you decide to go to the reggae concert?
(A) So, did you decide to go to the reggae concert?
(B) So did you, decide to go to the reggae concert?
(C) Correct as it is

---

34. Is this perhaps what, you were looking for?
(A) Is this perhaps, what you were looking for?
(B) Is this, perhaps, what you were looking for?
(C) Correct as it is

---

35. Oh I'd love to go to Paris!
(A) Oh, I'd love to go to Paris!
(B) Oh I'd love, to go to Paris!
(C) Correct as it is

---

36. Pradip asked "How many students will be attending the picnic?"
(A) Pradip asked, "How many students will be attending the picnic?"
(B) Pradip, asked "How many students will be attending the picnic?"
(C) Correct as it is

---

37. Do you really think, Fiona, that I might qualify?
(A) Do you really think Fiona, that I might qualify?
(B) Do you really think, Fiona that I might qualify?
(C) Correct as it is

---

38. "If we divide the job among us," said Ellen "we should finish quickly."
(A) "If we divide the job among us," said Ellen, "we should finish quickly."
(B) "If we divide the job among us" said Ellen, "we should finish quickly."
(C) Correct as it is

---

39. That pie, by the way, was for our Thanksgiving dinner.
(A) That pie, by the way was for our Thanksgiving dinner.
(B) That pie by the way was for our Thanksgiving dinner.
(C) Correct as it is

Which item shows the correct way to punctuate the underlined part of the sentence? In some cases, punctuation is not needed.

40. Maria added one quarter teaspoon of sugar to her hamster's daily food.
- **(A)** one-quarter teaspoon of sugar
- **(B)** one quarter-teaspoon of sugar
- **(C)** Correct as it is

---

41. Mr. Lowry, our ever supportive advisor, met with us often to discuss our projects.
- **(A)** Mr. Lowry, our ever-supportive advisor,
- **(B)** Mr. Lowry, our ever supportive-advisor,
- **(C)** Correct as it is

---

42. He always repeated this saying: "Never leave till tomorrow that which you can do today."
- **(A)** He always: repeated this saying "Never
- **(B)** He always repeated this saying; "Never
- **(C)** Correct as it is

---

43. Evie's great grandfather inspired her to study bird behavior.
- **(A)** Evie's great grand-father inspired her
- **(B)** Evie's great-grandfather inspired her
- **(C)** Correct as it is

---

44. Jess knows a lot about cars he investigated how the shape and weight of a race car affect its acceleration.
- **(A)** Jess knows a lot about cars; he investigated
- **(B)** Jess knows a lot about cars: he investigated
- **(C)** Correct as it is

---

45. Superior Awards went to Luis Lazo, Northmoor; Ichiko Kwan, Centerville; and Ty Stewart, East Knox.
- **(A)** Luis Lazo, Northmoor: Ichiko Kwan, Centerville; and Ty Stewart, East Knox.
- **(B)** Luis Lazo; Northmoor; Ichiko Kwan; Centerville; and Ty Stewart; East Knox.
- **(C)** Correct as it is

ADVANCED—FORM Y

Which sentence shows the correct use of underlining or quotation marks?

46. They went to see the Japanese animation film "Spirited Away."
(A) They went to see the Japanese animation film Spirited Away.
(B) They went to see the Japanese animation film Spirited Away.
(C) Correct as it is

---

47. Do you want to renew your subscription to Fish and Wildlife?
(A) Do you want to renew your subscription to Fish and Wildlife?
(B) Do you want to renew your subscription to "Fish and Wildlife?"
(C) Correct as it is

---

48. "Please stop humming," Bernice said, "or I'll have to ask you to leave."
(A) Please stop humming," Bernice said, "or I'll have to ask you to leave.
(B) "Please stop humming, Bernice said," or I'll have to ask you to leave.
(C) Correct as it is

---

49. Farm Scene with River is a charming painting by Grandma Moses.
(A) "Farm Scene with River" is a charming painting by Grandma Moses.
(B) Farm Scene with River is a charming painting by Grandma Moses.
(C) Correct as it is

---

50. "Be sure to find out when the movie will be over, Rachel's mom said."
(A) Be sure to find out when the movie will be over, "Rachel's mom said."
(B) "Be sure to find out when the movie will be over," Rachel's mom said.
(C) Correct as it is

---

51. Zadia did her book report on "The Adventures of Tom Sawyer by Mark Twain."
(A) Zadia did her book report on The Adventures of Tom Sawyer by Mark Twain.
(B) Zadia did her book report on "The Adventures of Tom Sawyer" by Mark Twain.
(C) Correct as it is

---

52. Nathan can play Red River Valley on his guitar.
(A) Nathan can play Red River Valley on his guitar.
(B) Nathan can play "Red River Valley" on his guitar.
(C) Correct as it is

ADVANCED—FORM Y ends on this page.

Student Worksheet **Placement Tests**

Name ______________________ Date __________

Form: ❑ X ❑ Y Test Level: ❑ Primary ❑ Intermediate ❑ Advanced

❑ Grammar	❑ Usage	❑ Mechanics
❑ Spelling	❑ Vocabulary	❑ Sentences
❑ Paragraphs	❑ Writing Process	❑ Research

1. ______	23. ______	45. ______	67. ______	89. ______	111. ______
2. ______	24. ______	46. ______	68. ______	90. ______	112. ______
3. ______	25. ______	47. ______	69. ______	91. ______	113. ______
4. ______	26. ______	48. ______	70. ______	92. ______	114. ______
5. ______	27. ______	49. ______	71. ______	93. ______	115. ______
6. ______	28. ______	50. ______	72. ______	94. ______	116. ______
7. ______	29. ______	51. ______	73. ______	95. ______	117. ______
8. ______	30. ______	52. ______	74. ______	96. ______	118. ______
9. ______	31. ______	53. ______	75. ______	97. ______	119. ______
10. ______	32. ______	54. ______	76. ______	98. ______	120. ______
11. ______	33. ______	55. ______	77. ______	99. ______	121. ______
12. ______	34. ______	56. ______	78. ______	100. ______	122. ______
13. ______	35. ______	57. ______	79. ______	101. ______	123. ______
14. ______	36. ______	58. ______	80. ______	102. ______	124. ______
15. ______	37. ______	59. ______	81. ______	103. ______	125. ______
16. ______	38. ______	60. ______	82. ______	104. ______	126. ______
17. ______	39. ______	61. ______	83. ______	105. ______	127. ______
18. ______	40. ______	62. ______	84. ______	106. ______	128. ______
19. ______	41. ______	63. ______	85. ______	107. ______	129. ______
20. ______	42. ______	64. ______	86. ______	108. ______	130. ______
21. ______	43. ______	65. ______	87. ______	109. ______	
22. ______	44. ______	66. ______	88. ______	110. ______	